CHASE RYDER

Game Day Decisions

Winning Strategies to Eliminate Emotion, Reduce Risk, and Beat the Odds in Sports Betting

This book was professionally typeset on Reedsy.
Find out more at reedsy.com

Contents

Introduction

Last Sunday, late in the game, Kareem Hunt (KC Chiefs) caught a swing pass in the flat. He was the last leg of the parlay, but I needed him to get 11 yards receiving. It for sure would be his last opportunity of the game. I was surprised, because he hadn't been targeted all game. So needless to say, I NEEDED those 11 yds to come on this particular play. And unfortunately, it looked like heartbreak on the horizon. But somehow, some way... Kareem stumbled forward and as he fell, he reached out 1 yard past the first down marker...

Hallelujah!

I hate the Chiefs, but this incredible gentleman unlocked the last leg of my parlay to the tune of $520! And, coupled with a separate bet that I cashed out early, my grand winnings for the day were almost $750. My risk was $45.

Wager **$25.00**   Payout **$520.00**

📶 FanCash **$1.08**   ⑤ **10% Profit Boost**

🔗 **Share Bet**

Travis Kelce 50+   -220
ALT Receiving Yards
NFL - Regular Season • Tampa Bay Buccaneers at Kansas City Chiefs
(Nov 4, 2024, 6:18pm)

Cade Otton 5+   -200
ALT Receptions
NFL - Regular Season • Tampa Bay Buccaneers at Kansas City Chiefs
(Nov 4, 2024, 6:18pm)

Kareem Hunt 50+   -250
ALT Rushing Yards
NFL - Regular Season • Tampa Bay Buccaneers at Kansas City Chiefs
(Nov 4, 2024, 6:18pm)

Over 17.5   -120
Kareem Hunt - Rushing Attempts
NFL - Regular Season • Tampa Bay Buccaneers at Kansas City Chiefs
(Nov 4, 2024, 6:18pm)

Over 55.5   +100
Cade Otton - Receiving Yards
NFL - Regular Season • Tampa Bay Buccaneers at Kansas City Chiefs
(Nov 4, 2024, 6:18pm)

Over 10.5   -120
Kareem Hunt - Receiving Yards
NFL - Regular Season • Tampa Bay Buccaneers at Kansas City Chiefs
(Nov 4, 2024, 6:18pm)

Deandre Hopkins 35+   -170
ALT Receiving Yards
NFL - Regular Season • Tampa Bay Buccaneers at Kansas City Chiefs
(Nov 4, 2024, 6:18pm)

Let's be real. Any way you slice it, that's a good day's work- more than

I make per day at my day job. But don't get it twisted; it *was* work. Not only the work to choose my parlay, but the discipline to practice proper risk management. And then, most importantly, the work to stay even-keel and logical with my decision to cash out early.

I'm sharing this with you because when you picked up this book or audiobook, undoubtedly, it's because you have some intrigue with the idea of sports betting (or, gambling, as the un-cool kids call it). Maybe you've been hearing all your buddies talking about their latest wins or just *howclose* they came to winning a $19,000! Maybe your team sucks and you're looking for a way to make some money while you suffer through your team's losing streak. Or MAYBE, you're the conservative type (that I used to be) that needs to make more money but can't afford to risk money betting unless it's a sure thing.

If that's you, I want you to know, I've got you covered. But you should also know that especially in this game, **there is no such thing as a sure thing**! But the good news is that *there is* such thing as **skill**, and **logic** that allows you to beat the odds more often than not.

As a beginner in your sports-betting journey, this book will be a game-changer for you, because the entire purpose of this book is to give you the mindset and the skills to stay even-keeled, emotionally, and to mitigate your risks as much as possible. With this information, you'll be better equipped to stay in the game long enough to experience frequent victories. Without it, chances are your finances, or your emotions (and probably both) will undoubtedly be burned sooner than later.

I hope that gives you some perspective. Now, let's get into it!

1

The Fundamentals of Smart Betting

F ull transparency: while the story I shared in the opening serves as a feel-good story, most sports bettors lose more than they win. I'm no different. There are no fool-proof methods or guarantees. This chapter should serve as a warning not to be swayed by the wrong indicators, because just like casino gamblers can become addicted to slot machines, people can become addicted to sports betting. It's fun, and the adrenaline rush can impair judgement. Even the near misses can create such a rush that you can't wait to try again.

That's why it's so important that you understand the fundamentals.

Sports betting is an art that requires a balance of knowledge, strategy, and discipline. While many view it as mere chance or entertainment, successful betting hinges on a solid foundation of smart principles. By understanding the basics, conducting thorough research, practicing proper risk management and adopting a long-term perspective, you can turn what might seem like a gamble into a calculated and rewarding activity.

Understanding the Basics

I won't assume anything regarding your knowledge and experience about sports betting. Understanding the basics means being clear on the foundational concepts of sports betting. Terms like *moneyline, point spread*, and *over/under* are the backbone of most wagers. For instance, the **moneyline** bet involves picking a winner, with odds indicating how much you can win relative to your stake. The **point spread** levels the playing field by assigning a handicap to the favorite team, requiring them to win by a certain margin. **Over/under** bets let you wager on the combined score of both teams, offering a different dimension to analyze.

Grasping these concepts ensures you're not betting blindly but rather making informed decisions based on the structure of the game and the odds presented.

Moneyline- When you bet the **moneyline** on a game/match, you're basically choosing which team will win. On most betting mobile applications, the moneyline is one of the most basic things to bet.

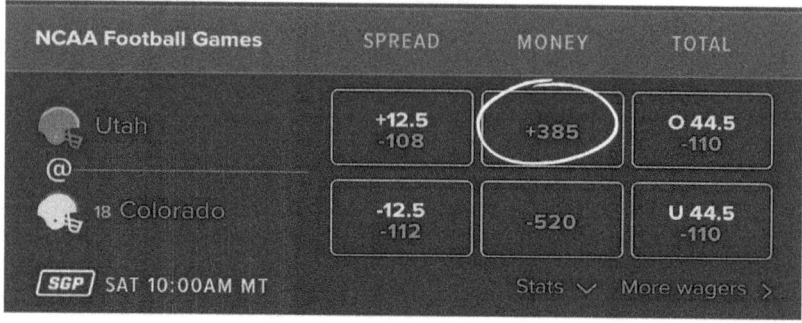

In this image, the bettor is choosing Utah to win the game. The +/- on the moneyline determines the odds. The example shows a "+" moneyline for Utah, meaning that they are not favored to win the match. This also means that with longer odds (think, longshot) you would earn significantly more money by choosing the underdog. If you placed $100 on Utah to win, you'd earn $385*. You wouldn't earn much money if you chose Colorado at -520 odds, because they are expected to win. In fact, you'd only win $19.23*. So again, if you see (+), that team is not favored. If you see (-), that team is favored. The higher the negative number, the less likely that the underdog pulls off the upset.

*= calculations determined by using a simple sports betting calculator

Point Spread- When you're making bets with the point spread, you're choosing how much a team will win or lose by. If the odds don't make sense to bet on a heavy favorite, you can typically find much better odds by choosing how badly they'll win.

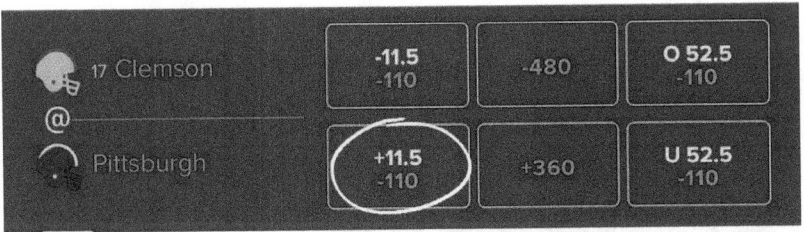

In this image, if the bettor had chosen #17 Clemson at -11.5, he/she is saying they believe that Clemson will win the game by at least 12 points. The indicator here again is the (+/-). Choosing the (+11.5) means the bettor is not necessarily saying they believe Pitt will WIN, but instead that Pitt will not LOSE by more than 12. Obviously, that's an interesting way to think about winning and losing, but it's a way to get more favorable odds for your money. In other words, if you chose the Clemson moneyline, a $100 bet would return you $20.83* if they win. However, if you choose Clemson -11.5, and they win by 12 points or more, your $100 bet would return $90.91. In fact, since they have the same odds, the same would be true if you chose Pitt +11.5 and they "cover the spread" by either winning outright or losing by 11 points or less.

*= calculations determined by using a simple sports betting calculator

Over/Under- The beautiful thing about sports betting is that you can get creative, because there are so many different things that you can bet on. But the over/under is the last of the major options. The over/under simply means that you can choose how many total points are scored.

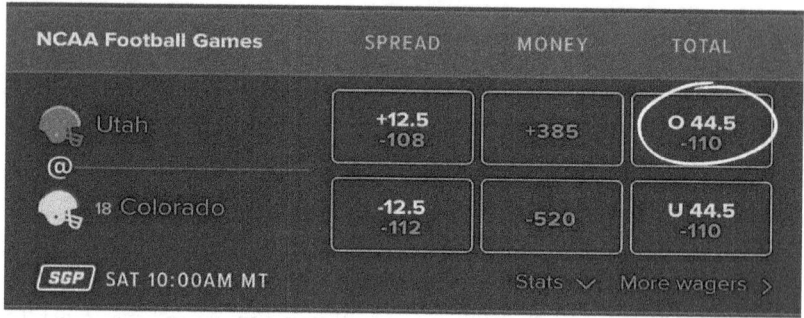

In this image, the bettor is not choosing a winner or point spread. Instead, they are choosing that the total amount of points scored will be 45 points or higher. Even though these numbers have a decimal, you must round up each number you're considering. If this bettor is correct, a $100 bet will return $90.91*. In this example, if the bettor chose the under, and the teams scored a combined 44 points or less, that same $100 bet would again return $90.91 because both options have the same odds.

*= calculations determined by using a simple sports betting calculator

There are a few more terms that you'll want to understand: *prop bets, straight bets and parlays.*

Prop Bets- A prop (or proposition) bet is a type of side wager on parts of a game or event that may have nothing to do with the final outcome. Money lines, over/unders and point spreads are examples of outcome wagers. Prop bets essentially are bets on individual/team stats or events within a game/match. Examples of popular prop bets range from picking the first player to record a basket in an NBA game to how many yards receiving a particular player gains during a game. Prop bets are extremely popular opportunities. Some prop bets are only permissible in certain states. For example, in some states, you cannot bet on individual stats in collegiate sports.

Straight Bets Vs. Parlays- When placing bets, you'll need to understand the terminology and difference between a straight bet and a parlay, and what it means to your overall betting strategy.

A straight bet is a simple bet that is not combined with any other bets. Examples of a straight bet could be a moneyline wager. Or a wager on the spread.

A parlay is a string of two or more straight bets, combined for stronger odds, and higher payouts.

The biggest differentiation is that with straight bets, each bet is considered separately. With a parlay, ALL bets (legs) within the parlay must win for the entire parlay to payout.

Ex: you could place three straight bets on the aforementioned games. If the Colorado game ends with over 45 points scored, you win that bet. If Pitt loses by 7, you win that bet also. If Colorado wins, you lose that bet. So, you end up winning 2 of 3.

However, if you'd placed all three of those as a parlay, and those same outcomes occurred, you would have lost the entire parlay and not won any money.

Do Your Homework

No betting strategy is bulletproof. There are so many different variables that can still sink the ship of a great bet; injury, blowouts, team gameplans, etc. Success in sports betting doesn't come from gut feelings or hunches—it's grounded in comprehensive research. In other words, beating the odds begins with a philosophy of educated guessing. So, if you don't have a good foundation of knowledge about the things you're betting on, chances are, the only thing you have going for you is the potential to get lucky.

A smart bettor's greatest tool is knowledge... This involves studying teams, players, and external factors such as injuries, weather conditions, and even travel schedules.

Trends and statistics also play a critical role. How has the team (or player) performed in recent games (or against certain teams)? Do they excel or struggle in specific conditions, like playing on the road or against a certain type of opponent? Analyzing historical data helps you identify patterns that might inform your betting decisions.

If you bet regularly and want to ensure higher probabilities of success, you'll want to take the time to do research, and not be blinded by attraction to shiny odds.

Practice Safe Bets

One of the most overlooked yet crucial aspects of smart betting is risk management. This refers to setting a fixed amount of money for betting (bankroll) and deciding how much to stake on each wager. That fixed amount of money should be a hard cap. A "hard cap" is simply you having the discipline to ONLY bet that amount of money, no matter what. Whatever amount you choose should be an amount that you are comfortably able to lose. I know that sounds pessimistic, but that's how successful bettors think. You MUST look at any money that you wager as money that's gone, no matter what. If you're wrong and you win, that's a pleasant development. But until then, consider the money gone. No different than if you spent money at a restaurant. So, if you need that money to pay your rent, it's not a great idea to use it on a wager. *EVEN THE SURE-THING BET!*

Why? Remember, there are no sure things.

Earlier this year, I had a 9-leg NFL parlay going, with bets spread over a wide range of games. Eight of those legs had already hit, and I only needed one more leg to hit. It was the afternoon game, and I had to wait. My sportsbook offered me an opportunity to cash out early for over $250. I was conflicted, because the $250 would've been a great day's work, but if I stayed in the bet for that last leg to hit, the payout would be $630. The last leg I needed was for a certain player (Rashee Rice) to have 50 yards receiving, and he'd been averaging about 96 yards per game. Basically, it was a sure thing.

What would you do? Cash out early and take the money, or stay in and get ALL the money?

Because this leg was a "sure thing", I stayed in. Next thing you know, the unimaginable happened. Patrick Mahomes threw an interception (believable), and as the defender attempted to return the ball for a touchdown, Patrick Mahomes lowered his head to tackle the guy, MISSED, and instead ran right into Rashee Rice's knee (un-believable). And so, just like that, there went the entire parlay, down the drain.

Did your jaw drop? Mine did. So did my heart. I couldn't believe it! Now, it's important to remember that I didn't *lose* $630- that wasn't mine to lose. I didn't even lose the $250, because again, that wasn't mine yet. I only lost my initial wager. But the point remains that even when it seems inevitable, there is no such thing as a "sure thing", so the amount you place as a wager must be an amount that you'd be ok to lose.

There is no shame in determining your budget for this, just like you would anything else in life. Don't let anybody peer pressure you into increasing your budget, because chances are, they're not going to help you pay your bills when your parlay fails. So, if your budget is $100, don't move past that until you get to a point where your finances wouldn't be ruined if you lost the entire $100. Got it?

Now, the second part of this risk management is give yourself a limit for each straight bet or parlay. A common rule of thumb is to bet only 1-5% of your total available.

For example, if your bankroll is $100, you should wager no more than $5 on a single bet. This approach minimizes the impact of losses and allows you to continue betting even during a losing streak. Recklessly wagering large sums or chasing losses is a surefire way to drain your funds quickly.

The Long Game

Your betting philosophy might be tied to your reason for betting in the first place. If you're in it for the entertainment and you just want to have some fun since your team sucks, then yes, maybe you can place some money on some fun bets and try to hit a jackpot.

If your goal is creating an income stream that has some level of consistency, then your philosophy should be centered around consistency and sustainability. A disciplined bettor understands that wins and losses are part of the process. Instead of focusing on immediate outcomes, adopt a long-term mindset.

This means avoiding impulsive bets driven by frustration or excitement. Even when you experience a string of losses, stick to your strategy and trust the process. By making calculated, rational bets over time, you increase your chances of being profitable in the long run.

The Bottom Line

Building a strong foundation for sports betting requires a commitment to understanding the basics, conducting thorough research, managing your bankroll wisely, and thinking strategically about your approach. It's not just about placing bets—it's about making informed decisions that reduce risk and maximize potential rewards.

By mastering these core principles, you set yourself apart from the average bettor who relies on luck. Instead, you become a strategist, prepared to navigate the unpredictable world of sports betting with confidence and control.

2

Eliminating Emotion from Your Bets

We're a few pages into this book and I've shared one feel-good betting story and one wtf-I-can't-believe-it story. Things are gonna happen. In the world of sports betting, emotion is both a powerful motivator and a dangerous pitfall. While the thrill of the game can be exhilarating, it can also cloud judgment, leading to impulsive decisions and unnecessary risks. Successful betting isn't about riding the emotional highs and lows—it's about staying objective, disciplined, and focused on long-term strategy. Eliminating emotion from your bets can improve your chances of consistent success.

The Pitfalls of Emotional Betting

Emotion-driven betting is one of the most common reasons people lose money in sports betting. Here are some emotion-driven scenarios to avoid:

- **Chasing Losses**: Some of the same behaviors that create bad gambling habits can affect sports bettors as well. Whether you're on a losing streak, or you've just experienced an emotional outcome like the one I shared with Rashee Rice getting injured, the temptation to place an impromptu, un-researched bet to "win it all back" can be overwhelming. This reactive behavior often leads to even greater losses, as it's driven by desperation rather than logic.

- **Bias Toward Favorite Teams**: This was one of the hardest things for me at first. I was making decisions on bets involving my favorite team based on my hopes and desires, instead of basing them on my research. Betting on teams or players you love can cloud your judgment. Your attachment might prevent you from seeing their weaknesses or evaluating their chances objectively. Betting is not for fans.

- **Revenge Betting**: (See: Chasing losses.) Losing a bet on a team or player may lead to placing another wager out of frustration, aiming to "get even." This emotional response rarely aligns with sound strategy.

Recognizing these emotional pitfalls is the first step in avoiding them. The next step is implementing strategies to maintain composure and make rational decisions.

Sticking to a Plan

The antidote to emotional betting is having a clear, well-defined plan that guides your decisions. A solid betting plan includes:

Setting Betting Rules: Decide in advance how much you will bet, what types of bets you'll place, and the maximum amount you're willing to lose in a day, week, or month. These boundaries act as guardrails to keep you on track.

Defining Objectives: Are you betting for entertainment, to supplement your income, or to make it a serious side hustle? Understanding your goals helps you approach betting with the right mindset and expectations.

Prioritizing Value Over Fun: Your betting plan should focus on finding value in odds rather than betting for excitement. For instance, placing a wager on a big underdog because it's thrilling might not align with a disciplined approach.

Detaching from Teams and Players

One of the hardest habits to break is emotional attachment to certain teams, players, or outcomes. This is especially challenging if you're a fan of a particular sport or team. However, successful betting requires separating fandom from analysis.

Avoid Betting on Your Favorite Team: If you can't evaluate your team objectively, it's best to avoid betting on their games altogether. Bias can lead to overly optimistic or pessimistic assessments of their performance.

- **Focus on Numbers, Not Names**: Rather than fixating on big-name players or teams, concentrate on statistics, trends, and other data. This shift helps you see the game from a betting perspective rather than a fan's viewpoint.

- **Learn to Say No**: ***THIS IS A HUGE DISCIPLINE*** During football season, I research bets for games on Thursday, Saturday, Sunday and Monday. But sometimes I need to stay away. Not every game is worth betting on, even if it features your favorite team or a marquee matchup. Exercising restraint is a hallmark of disciplined betting.

Practicing Discipline

Discipline is the backbone of emotion-free betting. Without it, even the best strategies and research can be undermined by impulsive decisions. Here are some ways to cultivate discipline:

- **Track Your Bets**: Keeping a detailed record of your bets, including the rationale behind each one, helps you stay accountable. Over time, this practice reveals patterns in your behavior, highlighting emotional decisions you can work to eliminate.

- **Set Time Limits**: Allocate specific times for researching and placing bets and avoid making spur-of-the-moment wagers. This prevents boredom or frustration from leading to poor decisions.

- **Take Breaks**: Step away from betting after a significant win or loss. A break allows you to reset emotionally and refocus on your strategy.

- **Celebrate Wins with Restraint**: While it's natural to feel good after a win, avoid letting the excitement influence your next bets. Stick to your plan and maintain perspective.

Techniques for Emotional Control

Even with the best intentions, emotions can still creep in. Incorporating specific techniques to stay calm and composed can help:

Mindfulness and Meditation: Practicing mindfulness can improve your ability to stay present and make rational decisions under pressure. Simple breathing exercises can help you refocus when emotions run high.

Visualization: Before placing a bet, visualize both the best and worst-case outcomes. This mental exercise prepares you for any result, reducing the emotional impact of a loss.

Accountability Partners: Share your betting plan with a trusted friend or fellow bettor. Having someone to discuss your decisions with can provide valuable perspective and deter impulsive choices.

Learning from Mistakes

No matter how disciplined you are, mistakes are inevitable. What sets successful bettors apart is their ability to learn from them. Instead of dwelling on losses, treat them as opportunities for growth.

- **Review Every Bet**: After each bet, analyze what went right or wrong. Was your research thorough? Did you stick to your plan? Identifying areas for improvement strengthens your future decisions.

- **Avoid Self-Blame**: Losses are part of the process. Even the best strategies won't guarantee wins. Accepting this reality helps you stay emotionally balanced.

- **Adjust, Don't Overhaul**: If you notice a flaw in your approach, make incremental adjustments rather than abandoning your entire strategy. Consistency is key.

Staying the Course

The path to becoming a successful sports bettor is a marathon, not a sprint. Eliminating emotion from your bets doesn't mean stripping away the enjoyment—it means channeling your passion into calculated decisions. By sticking to a plan, detaching from personal biases, and practicing discipline, you can make rational choices that increase your chances of long-term success.

Betting without emotion requires effort, but the rewards are worth it. You'll not only improve your results but also find greater satisfaction in the process, knowing you're approaching each bet with clarity and confidence.

3

Mitigating Risk

Sports betting, like any form of investment, carries inherent risks. The key to long-term success isn't eliminating these risks entirely but learning to manage and mitigate them effectively. Risk mitigation allows you to make informed decisions that protect your bankroll while maximizing your opportunities for profit.

Diversifying Your Bets

Diversification is a strategy borrowed from the world of finance, and it's just as applicable to sports betting. The principle is simple: don't put all your eggs in one basket.

Avoiding Single-Game Reliance: While betting on a single game can be thrilling, it also concentrates your risk. By spreading your wagers across multiple games or bet types, you reduce the impact of a single loss. For instance, rather than placing your entire bankroll on one team to win, you could diversify with a mix of moneyline, point spread, and over/under bets across different matchups.

Exploring Different Sports or Markets: If you primarily bet on one sport, consider branching out into others where you have knowledge or insights. Diversification can also mean exploring different betting markets, such as live betting or futures.

The Art of Value Betting

Value betting is a cornerstone of risk management and profitability. It involves identifying bets where the odds offered by the bookmaker are higher than the actual probability of the outcome occurring.

Calculating Implied Probability: To find value, convert the bookmaker's odds into implied probability. Compare this with your assessment of the event's likelihood. If your probability is higher, the bet may have value.

Focusing on Marginal Gains: Value betting often involves small, incremental profits rather than huge payouts. Over time, these add up, especially when combined with disciplined bankroll management.

Avoiding High-Risk Gambles

While high-risk bets like parlays and long-shot futures can be tempting due to their potential for large payouts, they rarely align with a smart betting strategy.

The Parlay Trap: One of my favorite things to talk about is the parlay trap. One of the most common things you hear bettors talking about is how they missed their parlay by one leg.

Parlays require multiple outcomes to go your way, significantly reducing your chances of winning. Even seasoned bettors limit their use of parlays to situations with clear value.

Managing the Upside vs. Downside: For every high reward bet, consider the potential impact on your bankroll if it doesn't pay off. Risking a large percentage of your bankroll on a single outcome can lead to long-term failure.

Setting Limits

One of the simplest ways to mitigate risk is to establish clear limits for yourself.

Stop-Loss Thresholds: Decide in advance how much you're willing to lose in a day, week, or month. Once you hit that limit, stop betting.

Profit Goals: Similarly, set a target for winnings. Knowing when to walk away after a good streak helps you lock in profits rather than risking them on emotional bets.

4

Developing a Winning Strategy

A winning strategy is the backbone of successful sports betting. While luck plays a role, consistent profitability comes from a structured approach rooted in research, analysis, and disciplined execution.

Finding Your Niche

The sports betting world is vast, encompassing numerous sports, leagues, and betting markets. Specializing in a specific area can give you a competitive edge.

Focus on What You Know: Start with sports or leagues you're already familiar with. Understanding the nuances of a specific game or team gives you a head start.

Identify Market Inefficiencies: Bookmakers can't always set perfect odds for every market. By specializing, you can spot discrepancies and exploit them for value.

Leveraging Data and Tools

In today's data-driven world, information is power. Successful bettors use data and analytical tools to inform their decisions.

Tracking Trends and Statistics: Historical data can reveal patterns that help predict future outcomes. Look for trends in team performance, player stats, or situational factors like home-field advantage.

Using Technology: Betting tools, such as odds comparison websites and analytics platforms, can help you make more informed decisions. Advanced tools can even calculate probabilities and suggest value bets.

Tracking Performance

Maintaining a record of your bets is essential for refining your strategy and identifying areas for improvement.

Keeping a Betting Journal: Record every bet you place, including the type of bet, the odds, your rationale, and the result. Over time, this journal becomes a treasure trove of insights.

Analyzing Outcomes: Review your wins and losses to understand what worked and what didn't. This helps you fine-tune your approach and avoid repeating mistakes.

Timing Your Bets

When you place your bets can be just as important as what you bet on.

Monitoring Line Movements: Odds can shift due to factors like injuries, weather, or public betting trends. Keeping an eye on these changes allows you to act when value presents itself.

Avoiding Last-Minute Bets: Rushed decisions often lead to poor judgment. Allow yourself ample time to analyze games and place bets thoughtfully.

5

Staying in Control

Sports betting is as much a mental game as it is a numbers game. Staying in control—both financially and emotionally—is critical for long-term success.

Recognizing Problematic Patterns

Uncontrolled betting habits can quickly spiral into a problem. Recognizing the warning signs is the first step to staying in control.

Signs of Emotional Betting: Placing bets out of frustration, chasing losses, or betting on every game to "stay in the action" are red flags.

Acknowledging Addiction Risks: If betting begins to interfere with your personal, financial, or professional life, it's time to take a step back and seek help if necessary.

Building a Betting Routine

A structured routine helps you approach betting with discipline and focus.

Research First: Allocate time to gather information and analyze games before placing bets.

Set Limits on Betting Time: Avoid spending excessive hours betting, as it can lead to fatigue and impulsive decisions.

Staying Inspired but Grounded

Betting can be exciting, but it's important to stay grounded and avoid being swept away by emotions.

Focus on the Process: Rather than fixating on immediate wins or losses, trust your strategy and enjoy the process of making informed decisions.

Celebrate Success Modestly: Winning streaks are worth acknowledging, but they shouldn't lead to overconfidence or reckless betting.

Taking Breaks

Sometimes, the best way to stay in control is to step away.

Cool-Off Periods: After a significant win or loss, taking a break helps you reset emotionally and prevents rash decisions.

Maintaining Balance: Remember that sports betting should complement your life, not dominate it. Prioritize other hobbies and responsibilities.

6

Conclusion: The Final Whistle

S ports betting is a fascinating combination of strategy, discipline, and excitement. As we wrap up this journey, it's important to take stock of the tools and principles we've covered—building a smart foundation, eliminating emotion, mitigating risks, developing winning strategies, and staying in control. These are the cornerstones of success in betting, guiding you to approach every wager with confidence and clarity.

Remember, sports betting is more than just luck. It's about preparation and smart decision-making. Those who succeed don't rely on hunches or gut feelings—they rely on research, planning, and a disciplined mindset. While the outcomes of games are unpredictable, your approach doesn't have to be. With consistent effort, you can create a betting process that's both enjoyable and profitable over time.

The Power of Patience and Discipline

Patience and discipline are critical traits for anyone hoping to find long-term success in sports betting. It's tempting to chase quick wins or bet impulsively when emotions run high, but staying the course and sticking to a well-thought-out strategy is the path to sustained success. Every bet should align with your overall plan, supported by analysis and logic.

It's also important to remember that success doesn't happen overnight. The most successful bettors understand that sports betting is a long game. Wins and losses are both part of the process, and each one carries valuable lessons. By committing to steady, calculated progress, you'll build a foundation that stands the test of time.

Betting as a Balanced Pursuit

For most, sports betting is a way to enhance the enjoyment of watching games or an intellectual challenge to outsmart the odds. However, it should never overshadow the other important aspects of your life. A balanced approach ensures that betting remains a positive and enriching experience, not a source of stress or over-extension.

Stay Connected and Continue Growing

One of the joys of sports betting is the community it fosters. Engaging with other bettors, sharing experiences, and discussing strategies can elevate your own approach. The world of sports betting evolves constantly, and learning from others can keep you ahead of the game. Whether through forums, social media groups, or industry resources, stay connected to keep improving.

The Next Step in Your Journey

As you move forward, keep in mind that this book is just the beginning of your sports betting story. There will always be more to learn, markets to explore, and strategies to refine. With the insights and tools, you've gained here, you're now equipped to approach each bet with greater understanding and control.

If you've found this book helpful, I have one small favor to ask. Please consider leaving a review to share your thoughts. Reviews not only help others discover this guide but also allow me to continue improving and providing value to readers like you. Your feedback means the world to me and helps ensure that this community of smart bettors continues to grow.

Thank you for choosing *Game Day Decisions*.

Good luck in all your betting endeavors, and may your strategies lead you to success!

7

Game Day Bonuses

As a beginner in sports betting, you're likely eager to dive in and start placing bets. To set yourself up for success, it's crucial to start with a solid foundation. In this bonus section, we'll cover ten quick tips for beginners and highlight some valuable resources and tools to help you on your journey.

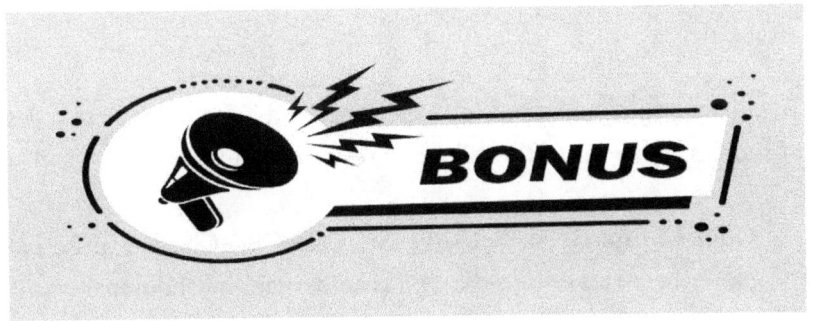

Top 10 Quick Tips for Beginners

1. **Start Small**: Begin with small bets to minimize risk as you learn the ropes.
2. **Set a Budget**: Determine how much you're willing to spend and stick to it.
3. **Focus on One Sport**: Specialize in a sport you know well to improve your chances of making informed decisions.
4. **Do Your Research**: Analyze teams, players, and matchups before placing any bets.
5. **Avoid Parlays Initially**: While tempting, parlays are high-risk and better suited for experienced bettors.
6. **Understand Odds**: Learn to read and interpret odds to identify potential value
7. **Keep Emotions in Check**: Avoid betting on your favorite team unless the data supports it.
8. **Track Your Bets**: Maintain a record of your wagers to evaluate your performance and identify patterns.
9. **Stay Updated**: Follow the latest news and developments in your chosen sport to make timely decisions.
10. **Take Breaks**: Regularly step away to maintain perspective and avoid burnout.

Resources and Tools

To enhance your sports betting experience and improve your chances of success, make use of the following resources and tools:

- **Odds Comparison Websites:** Sites like OddsChecker or BetExplorer help you find the best odds across multiple bookmakers.

- **Statistical Databases:** Platforms like Sports Reference and ESPN offer comprehensive stats for in-depth analysis.

- **Betting Calculators:** Tools like arbitrage calculators and implied probability converters simplify complex calculations.

- **News and Analysis Sites:** Websites like The Athletic and Bleacher Report provide expert insights and breaking news.

- **Mobile Apps:** Apps like Action Network allow you to track your bets and access real-time updates on odds and scores.

With these tips and resources, you'll be well-equipped to navigate the world of sports betting as a beginner. Remember, success in betting is a marathon, not a sprint. Stay disciplined, informed, and patient as you develop your skills.

Resources and References

The information presented in *Game Day Decisions* is based on general principles of sports betting, financial risk management, psychology, and industry knowledge. While no direct quotes or proprietary material from specific sources were used, the following types of references informed the content and methodology presented in this book:

General References

- **Sports Betting Fundamentals:** General knowledge from sports betting guides and articles discussing betting types, odds calculation, and strategies. Resources from odds comparison and sports statistics websites like OddsChecker and Sports Reference.

- **Psychology of Decision-Making:** Insights on behavioral economics and cognitive biases, such as the work of Daniel Kahneman (*Thinking, Fast and Slow*) and Richard Thaler (*Nudge*).

- **Risk Management Principles:** Basic principles of financial risk management, including bankroll management and diversification, which are adapted for the context of sports betting.

- **Gambling Addiction and Control Strategies:** Guidance from organizations like the National Council on Problem Gambling (NCPG) on recognizing and addressing problematic gambling behaviors.

- **Sports Analytics and Tools:** Data-driven approaches inspired by sports analytics methodologies used in professional sports organizations and betting circles.

About the Author

Chase Ryder is a seasoned sports betting enthusiast with over a decade of experience navigating the unpredictable world of wagers and odds. A strategic thinker and disciplined bettor, Chase has spent years refining his approach to sports betting, focusing on calculated risk management, emotional control, and data-driven decision-making.

Chase's journey began with a love for sports and a curiosity about the betting strategies behind the headlines. Through trial, error, and relentless learning, he developed a system that prioritizes logic over luck, enabling him to consistently outperform the average bettor. His insights blend a deep understanding of sports analytics with practical advice for staying grounded, making him a trusted voice for beginners and seasoned bettors alike.

When he's not analyzing games or placing bets, Chase shares his knowledge through writing, teaching others how to approach sports betting as a skillful and enjoyable pursuit. *Game Day Decisions* is the culmination of his experience, offering readers actionable strategies to eliminate emotion, reduce risk, and find success in the ever-evolving world of sports betting.

Chase lives by the mantra, "Bet smarter, not harder," and he's passionate about helping others enjoy the thrill of betting responsibly while maximizing their potential for success.

www.ingramcontent.com/pod-product-compliance
Lightning Source LLC
Chambersburg PA
CBHW070136230526
45472CB00004B/1553